The Countries

Bulgaria

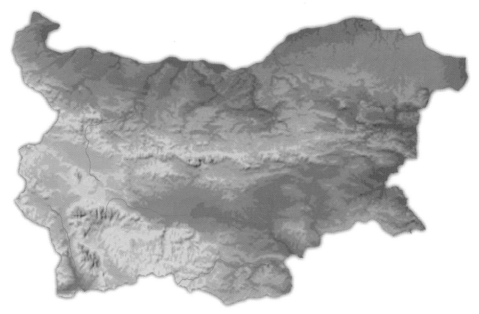

Kristin Van Cleaf
ABDO Publishing Company

visit us at
www.abdopublishing.com

Published by ABDO Publishing Company, 8000 West 78th Street, Edina, Minnesota 55439.
Copyright © 2008 by Abdo Consulting Group, Inc. International copyrights reserved in all
countries. No part of this book may be reproduced in any form without written permission from the
publisher. The Checkerboard Library™ is a trademark and logo of ABDO Publishing Company.

Printed in the United States.

Interior Photos: Alamy pp. 5, 13, 18, 23, 31; AP Images pp. 6, 8, 12, 24, 30, 33, 35;
    Corbis pp. 11, 12; Getty Images p. 37; Peter Arnold pp. 16, 19, 21, 27, 29

Editors: Rochelle Baltzer, Tamara L. Britton
Art Direction & Maps: Neil Klinepier

Library of Congress Cataloging-in-Publication Data

Van Cleaf, Kristin, 1976-
 Bulgaria / Kristin Van Cleaf.
    p. cm. -- (The countries)
 Includes bibliographical references and index.
 ISBN 978-1-59928-781-2
 1. Bulgaria--Juvenile literature. I. Title.

 DR55.V36 2007
 949.9--dc22
                                                                    2007010178

Contents

Zdraveite!

Hello from Bulgaria! Bulgaria lies on the Balkan Peninsula in eastern Europe. It borders the Black Sea. Bulgaria's land is known for its majestic mountains, beautiful beaches, and the scent of its Valley of Roses.

For many centuries, Bulgaria struggled for independence. **Byzantine**, **Ottoman**, and **communist** rule all shaped the country's development. But, Bulgarians have kept their **culture** and language alive throughout years of hardship. Their traditional songs, dances, and other arts and crafts still endure.

After **World War II**, Bulgaria had communist and **socialist** governments. Today, Bulgaria is a **parliamentary democracy** and a member of the **European Union (EU)**. Together, Bulgarians and their government are working to make Bulgaria a great place to work and live!

Zdraveite *from Bulgaria!*

Fast Facts

OFFICIAL NAME: Republic of Bulgaria
CAPITAL: Sofia

LAND
- Area: 42,823 square miles (110,910 sq km)
- Mountain Ranges: Balkan, Sredna, Rhodope, Pirin, Rila
- Highest Point: Musala Peak 9,596 feet (2,925 m)
- Major Rivers: Danube, Maritsa, Iskŭr, Struma, Arda, Yantra

PEOPLE
- Population: 7,322,858 (July 2007 estimate)
- Major Cities: Sofia, Plovdiv, Varna
- Languages: Bulgarian (official), Turkish, Romany
- Religions: Bulgarian Orthodoxy, Islam, other Christian

GOVERNMENT
- Form: Parliamentary democracy
- Head of State: President
- Head of Government: Prime minister
- Legislature: National Assembly
- Nationhood: March 3, 1878

ECONOMY
- Agricultural Products: Vegetables, fruits, tobacco, wine, wheat, barley, sunflowers, sugar beets, livestock
- Mining Products: Coal, copper, lead, zinc, kaolin, salt, pyrite
- Manufactured Products: Textiles, machinery, chemicals, food, metal products
- Money: Lev (1 lev = 100 stotinki)

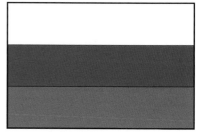

Bulgaria's flag

A sample of a 100 lev bill

Timeline

681	The First Bulgarian Empire forms
860s	Methodius and Cyril create the Bulgarian alphabet
864	Eastern Orthodoxy becomes Bulgaria's official religion
1014	Byzantine emperor Basil II defeats the Bulgarians
1185	Ivan and Peter Asen lead a revolt; the Second Bulgarian Empire forms
1396	The Ottoman Empire takes control of Bulgaria
1876	Bulgarians stage the unsuccessful April Uprising
1877	Russia declares war on the Ottoman Empire
1878	Bulgaria wins limited independence
1908	Ferdinand I declares Bulgaria's independence
1912	The Balkan League defeats the Ottoman Empire in the First Balkan War
1913	Bulgaria loses the Second Balkan War
1944	The Soviet Union invades Bulgaria
1990	Communists lose power in Bulgaria
2004	Bulgaria joins NATO
2007	Bulgaria joins the European Union

Bulgaria's History

Present-day Bulgaria was occupied by Thracians in ancient times. Eventually, Greeks and Persians took over. Romans conquered the area in about 40 BC.

In the AD 500s, Slavic tribes entered the region. They formed communities and farmed the land. In the 600s, the Bulgars conquered the area. In time, these two **cultures** united.

A Thracian king's gold mask

In 681, **Khan** Asparukh formed the First Bulgarian Empire. He and later khans expanded Bulgaria's territory. In 811, the Bulgarians conquered the **Byzantines**. Afterward, Bulgaria enjoyed a period of peace.

The Bulgarian Empire continued to develop. In 864, Khan Boris I became Christian. He made Eastern **Orthodoxy** the country's official religion. His son Simeon I became khan in 893. Simeon encouraged art and the building of churches and palaces. He also supported the translation of Greek literature into the Bulgar language.

When Simeon died in 927, Bulgaria's power began to weaken. In 1014, **Byzantine** emperor Basil II defeated the Bulgarians. He ordered 15,000 prisoners blinded. Because of this, he became known as "Basil, Slayer of the Bulgars."

Bulgaria remained under Byzantine rule until 1185. Then, brothers Ivan and Peter Asen led a revolt. Bulgaria gained independence and formed the Second Bulgarian Empire. Ivan became ruler in 1218 and led the empire until 1241.

After Ivan's death, internal conflict and attacks by northern Mongols weakened the country. In the mid-1300s, Bulgaria suffered attacks by the **Ottoman Empire**. The Ottomans slowly gained Bulgarian territory. In 1396, Bulgaria again lost its independence.

The Ottomans practiced Islam. But, they did not force most Bulgarians to become **Muslim**. However, Christians were treated as second-class citizens. They had to pay taxes to the Ottomans, including the Blood Tax. This required a certain number of Christian youths to become Muslim and serve in the Ottoman army.

In the 1600s, the **Ottoman Empire** suffered military defeats, as well as **economic** troubles. It began to weaken. The Bulgarians staged several uprisings but remained under Ottoman rule.

However, a **cultural** renaissance had begun in Bulgaria. In 1762, a monk named Paisii Hilendarski wrote *A Sloveno-Bulgarian History*. It encouraged Bulgarians to have pride in their culture. This led to the opening of new Bulgarian schools. By the 1870s, about 2,000 schools provided free education to young Bulgarians.

This cultural rebirth extended to the country's traditional religion. The Bulgarian **Orthodox** Church regained its independence in 1870.

Still, Bulgarians longed to be free of Ottoman rule. So in 1876, Bulgarians revolted again in the April Uprising. However, the Ottoman army crushed the revolt. Nearly 15,000 Bulgarians died. This became known as the Bulgarian Horrors.

Europeans were outraged by this savagery. They proposed a series of reforms to prevent future violence. But the Ottomans refused to cooperate. So in 1877, Russia declared war on the Ottoman Empire.

Bulgarians fought alongside the Russian troops. They won in 1878, and the **Ottomans** signed the Treaty of San Stefano. This treaty granted Bulgaria limited independence.

In 1879, the Bulgarians wrote a **constitution** and created a **parliament**. The parliament chose a German named Alexander of Battenberg as Bulgaria's first prince.

Ferdinand I

The country's next ruler, Ferdinand I, declared Bulgaria independent in 1908. In 1912, Bulgaria joined the **Balkan League**. That same year, the league defeated the Ottoman Empire in the First **Balkan War**.

After the war, Bulgaria did not receive the land it had hoped for. So in June 1913, Bulgaria attacked the other league members in the Second Balkan War. It was quickly defeated.

During **World War I**, Bulgaria joined the **Central powers**. Ferdinand hoped to regain land lost in the Balkan Wars. But the Central powers did not win the war. Ferdinand stepped down, and his son Boris III became leader.

Boris III

In 1919, Bulgaria lost more land in the Treaty of Neuilly. The treaty also required Bulgaria to pay the winning countries for their war expenses. In the next years, Bulgaria endured political and **economic** troubles. The nation had several

Georgi Dimitrov

leaders. Then, the **Great Depression** caused further suffering.

During **World War II**, Bulgaria again sided with Germany. On September 8, 1944, the Soviet Union invaded Bulgaria. The next day, Bulgarian **communists** overthrew the government. The ruling family fled in 1946. Then, Georgi Dimitrov became head of the government. The next year, Bulgaria created a **constitution** similar to the Soviet Union's.

Todor Zhivkov became the country's leader in 1954. He held that position for 35 years. Under his rule, Bulgaria's economy improved. However by the 1960s, the country still lacked many basic goods and services.

Todor Zhivkov

In the 1980s, Soviet leader Mikhail Gorbachev reformed the Soviet Union's government. In response, Bulgarians demanded similar freedoms and **democracy**. So in 1990, the **communists** gave up power. The people elected Zhelyu Zhelev as president in 1992. He led a more moderate **socialist** government.

Simeon II

But the **economy** did not improve. Prices increased, and fuel was in short supply. In the 1996 elections, Bulgarians rejected the socialist government. Then in 2001, a political party led by the exiled king Simeon II won control of the National Assembly. Later, he became prime minister.

Today, Bulgarians continue working to improve their country. In 2004, Bulgaria joined **NATO**. And in January 2007, Bulgaria was accepted into the **EU**.

Mountains and Streams

Bulgaria is located in southeastern Europe. It lies south of Romania and north of Greece and Turkey. Macedonia and Serbia share Bulgaria's western border. The country's eastern border is on the Black Sea.

Bulgaria's land is divided into several regions. The Danubian Plain lies in the north. It runs south from the Danube River to the Balkan Mountains. The Danube is one of Bulgaria's most important rivers. It provides shipping, fishing, and **irrigation**. Other major rivers in Bulgaria include the Maritsa, Iskŭr, Struma, Arda, and Yantra.

South of the Danubian Plain, the Balkan Mountains extend east to west. Farther south lay the Sredna Mountains. Between these mountain ranges is the Kazanlŭk (kah-zahn-LUHK) **Basin**. It is also called the Valley of Roses.

The Thracian Plain lies south of the Sredna Mountains. South of this are the Rhodope, Pirin, and Rila mountains. Bulgaria's tallest mountain, Musala Peak, is in the Rilas. It is 9,596 feet (2,925 m) high. The famous Rila Monastery is also located there.

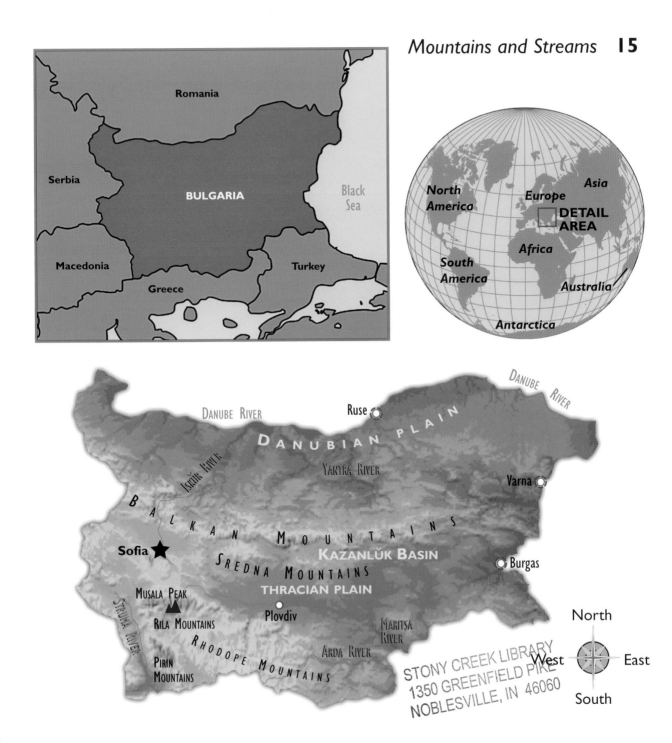

Romania

Serbia

BULGARIA

Black
Sea

Macedonia

Greece

Turkey

North
America

Europe

Asia

DETAIL
AREA

South
America

Africa

Australia

Antarctica

DANUBE RIVER

DANUBE RIVER

Ruse

DANUBIAN PLAIN

ISKŬR RIVER

YANTRA RIVER

Varna

BALKAN MOUNTAINS

KAZANLŬK BASIN

Sofia

SREDNA MOUNTAINS

Burgas

THRACIAN PLAIN

STRUMA RIVER

Musala Peak

Plovdiv

RILA MOUNTAINS

MARITSA
RIVER

RHODOPE MOUNTAINS

ARDA RIVER

PIRIN
MOUNTAINS

North

West   East

South

Much of Bulgaria has a moderate climate. The Danubian Plain has cold winters and hot, **humid** summers. Farther south, the Rhodopes have cool, moist winters. Summers there are hot and dry.

On average, Bulgaria receives 25 inches (65 cm) of rain each year. However, more than 40 inches (100 cm) may fall each year in the mountains. In winter, light snow falls in the lowlands. Snow falls more heavily in the mountains.

Musala Peak

Rainfall

AVERAGE YEARLY RAINFALL

Inches		Centimeters
Under 20		Under 50
20–40		50–100
40–60		100–150
Over 60		Over 150

Rain

North

West — East

South

Temperature

AVERAGE TEMPERATURE

Fahrenheit		Celsius
Over 65°		Over 18°
54°–65°		12°–18°
43°–54°		6°–12°
32°–43°		0°–6°
21°–32°		-6°–0°
Below 21°		Below -6°

Winter

Summer

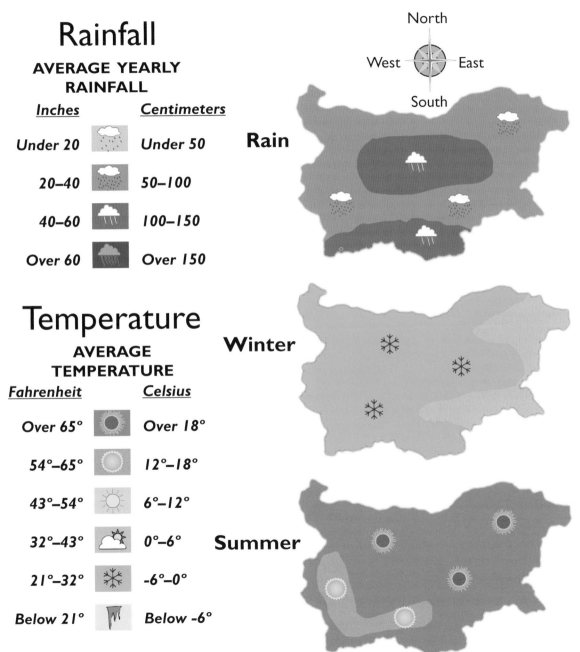

Wild Bulgaria

Bulgaria's diverse land is home to a variety of plants and animals. More than 250 distinctive plants grow there.

The climate and soil in the Valley of Roses is perfect for growing roses. Bulgaria's roses produce plentiful amounts of high-quality oil.

Some of the most common are Rila primroses, Rhodopean tulips, Balkan violets, and Bulgarian blackberries.

In the mountains, beech, oak, and pine trees cover the land. Wild mushrooms grow in these forests. Fruits such as raspberries, strawberries, blueberries, and blackberries are also found in these woods. Herbs and briars grow there, too.

Thousands of animal species live among the plant life. Some of them are rare. The country works to protect these animals and preserve

Pelicans find safety in the Srebarna Nature Reserve, a bird sanctuary near the Danube River.

the country's wildlife. So, animals such as stags, deers, goats, pelicans, quails, and pheasants live in reserves.

To further preserve their land and wildlife, Bulgarians have created the Rila, Pirin, and Central Balkan national parks. The country is also home to nature parks, as well as other protected areas.

The Republic of Bulgaria

Bulgaria's government is a **parliamentary democracy**. Its **constitution** guarantees freedom of speech, religion, and the press. Citizens who are at least 18 years old can vote to choose the country's leaders.

The National Assembly is Bulgaria's legislature. Bulgarians elect its 240 members to serve four-year terms. The legislature raises taxes, approves treaties, and passes and changes laws.

The prime minister is the head of the government. The political party with the most assembly members chooses the prime minister. He or she chooses a cabinet called the Council of Ministers. Together, they organize government policies and put them into action.

Bulgaria's president is the head of state. Citizens cast their vote for president every five years. The president organizes elections and is in charge of national security and the military.

Bulgaria's parliament building (right), *with the Alexander Nevsky Cathedral in the distance*

The Judicial Council runs Bulgaria's judicial branch. This system includes the Supreme Administrative Court and the Supreme Court of Appeals. Local courts, appeals courts, and military courts are also part of the judicial branch.

Bulgaria is divided into 28 regions called oblasts. Each oblast has a governor that is named by the Council of Ministers. Cities and towns have elected councils run by a mayor.

Bulgarians

Bulgaria's population is mostly Bulgarian. About 10 percent of the people are Turks. Other citizens are Romanian, Greek, Armenian, Roma, and Russian.

The country's people speak different **dialects** of Bulgarian. Bulgarian is the official language. It is similar to Russian and other Slavic languages. And, it is written in the Cyrillic alphabet. Some Bulgarians also speak Turkish or Romany.

Bulgarians enjoy freedom of religion. About 90 percent of the people are Bulgarian **Orthodox**. Some practice Islam or other Christian faiths. Others practice no religion.

Traditionally, Bulgarians lived in rural areas. But when the **communists** came to power, industrial growth created jobs in the cities. So, people moved to cities to work in factories. Most people still live in city apartments.

Those still living in rural areas don't often have indoor plumbing or furnaces. However, the government has been working to improve these conditions. It has paved roads and established electricity and telephone services in these areas.

*A traditional
Bulgarian home*

In Bulgaria, both men and women work. But, the unstable **economy** has affected the job market. Jobs can be hard to find and don't always pay well. There are shortages of food and housing, too.

Bulgarian schoolboys practice their computer skills

To improve these conditions and compete in the **EU**, Bulgarians focus on education. The government runs most of the schools. Children attend elementary school for eight years. Then they move on to high school. Afterward, students may attend any of several universities, **vocational** schools, or other specialty schools.

Bulgarians also find time to enjoy with family and friends. Often, these gatherings involve food. *Shopska* salad is made with cucumbers, tomatoes, peppers, parsley, and sheep's cheese. *Kavarma* is a casserole of pork, onions, and mushrooms. Yogurt is also a Bulgarian specialty.

Tarator

A delicious creamy soup made with yogurt. On a hot day, try adding an ice cube to each bowl before serving!

- 1 pound plain yogurt
- 1 cucumber, peeled and finely chopped
- 4 tablespoons olive oil
- 2 tablespoons fresh dill, finely chopped
- 1 1/2 cups cold water
- 2 garlic cloves, crushed
- 1 teaspoon salt
- 1/2 cup walnuts, finely chopped

In a large bowl, mix yogurt and water until smooth. Add remaining ingredients and stir well. Serve at once.

AN IMPORTANT NOTE TO THE CHEF: Always have an adult help with the preparation and cooking of food. Never use kitchen utensils or appliances without adult permission and supervision.

LANGUAGE

English	Bulgarian
Hello	Здравейте (zdra-VEHY-teh)
Good-bye	Довиждане (doh-VIHZH-da-neh)
Yes	Да (da)
No	Не (neh)
Please	Моля (MOH-lya)
Thank you	благодаря (bla-goh-dar-YA)

Making Money

When **communist** rule ended, Bulgaria's **economy** was unstable. Eventually, the government returned ownership of many businesses to individuals. The economy has slowly improved since then.

Bulgaria's most successful companies produce cloth, machinery, chemicals, food, and metal products. Much of the nation's manufacturing technology is old. So, the government provides these industries with financial assistance.

Many Bulgarians work in the mining industry. They dig coal, copper, lead, zinc, kaolin, salt, and pyrite from the land.

About one-fourth of Bulgarians are farmers. They grow wheat, corn, barley, oats, rye, and rice. Other important crops are apples, grapes, potatoes, pears, sugar beets, watermelons, and tomatoes. Farmers also raise cattle, chickens, goats, and pigs.

The service industry employs about one-third of Bulgarians. Education, health care, and other social and personal services provide the most jobs. People also work in stores, hotels, and restaurants.

Bulgaria trades with Germany, Greece, Russia, Italy, the United Kingdom, and the United States. The country's main imports are fuel, machinery, and metals. Its main exports are rose oil, machinery, and fruits and fruit products.

The Marina Royal Palace is one of the many resorts along Bulgaria's Black Sea coast. Vacationing tourists from all over the world add important leva to Bulgaria's economy.

Splendid Cities

Bulgaria's capital and largest city is Sofia. It lies in western Bulgaria in the Balkan Mountains. Sofia is home to the National Assembly and the former royal palace. The Cyril and Methodius National Library and the Ivan Vazov National Theater and Opera House are also located there.

The University of Sofia is the country's oldest. It includes the Bulgarian Academy of Science and the Academy of Agricultural Science. The city's old quarter has the tiny Saint George's Church, which was built in Roman times. The Alexander Nevsky Cathedral stands in the center of Sofia.

Plovdiv is the second-largest city. It lies in south central Bulgaria, on the Maritsa River. A city has stood there since the 400s BC. Many Roman buildings survive there, too. Plovdiv hosts an international trade fair every year.

Bulgaria's third-largest city is Varna. It sits on a bluff above the Black Sea. It is Bulgaria's most important port. The city has an oceanography institute, a naval academy, and several universities. Tourists enjoy Varna's historic buildings and seaside resorts. The Aladzha Monastery is also popular with visitors.

The Alexander Nevsky Cathedral is Europe's largest Orthodox church. It was built to honor the Russian troops who died liberating Bulgaria from the Ottoman Empire.

Staying Connected

Under **communist** rule, the government controlled Bulgaria's communications. But today, Bulgarians can communicate freely. Most have a radio and a television. Radio programs are often broadcast in several languages. Bulgarian National Television provides news, sports, children's programs, and documentaries. More than 2 million Bulgarians use the Internet.

*A Bulgarian couple reading a newspaper called **Trud**, which means "work" in English.*

Bulgarians also enjoy the freedom to travel, and 27,361 miles (44,033 km) of roads unite them. The European International Highway connects Bulgaria to Turkey. But, few citizens can afford cars. So, trains transport people and goods on the nation's 2,668 miles (4,294 km) of railways.

The Danube River is Bulgaria's main inland waterway. The Black Sea is also used for shipping and travel. Both allow national and international transport. Some of Bulgaria's larger ports are located in the cities Ruse, Varna, and Burgas.

Bulgaria has more than 200 airports. The main airport is in Sofia. It has two terminals and accommodates most of Bulgaria's air travel. Other major airports are located in Burgas and Varna.

A Bulgaria Airlines airplane

Celebrate!

Bulgarians observe many traditions. On March 1, they celebrate Baba Marta. Bulgarians wear a pair of red and white dolls called *martenitza*. People put them away once they see a stork, the first sign of spring.

The ancient Kukeri carnival also takes place in March. To celebrate, people wear furs, decorated masks, or traditional clothing. Some also wear bells around their waists. The bells drive away evil spirits and welcome the growing season.

May 21 is the day of Saints Constantine and Elena. The event marks the beginning of summer. Bulgarians celebrate with *Nestinarstvo*, or fire dancing. Fire dancers walk barefoot over hot coals!

In the 860s, Saints Methodius and Cyril developed the Bulgarian alphabet. On May 24, these two brothers are honored on the Day of Culture.

June brings the Festival of Roses. Bulgarians harvest rose petals to make rose oil, which is used in perfume. At the same time, they celebrate with festivals and parades.

Bulgaria's national holiday is on March 3. Liberation Day celebrates the country's independence from the **Ottoman Empire** in 1878. Independence Day, on September 22, celebrates the country's 1908 independence.

Children celebrate the Day of Culture by placing flowers on a monument to Saints Cyril and Methodius.

Bulgarian Culture

Modern Bulgarians continue to celebrate their **culture**. Traditional art, music, and dance are important to them. So, they work to preserve their **folklife**.

Traditional artisans craft items from clay. Potters make pots, baking dishes, bowls, and plates. They also make decorated jugs and vases for weddings and other ceremonies. Colorful roses, flowers, and animal figures often decorate their work.

Folk music features singing accompanied by traditional folk instruments. These include the bagpipe, the flute, the violin, the guitar, and the drum. Folk music often accompanies folk dancing.

Some folk dances are done with a partner. Others are performed in a circle or a line. The steps are fast and difficult! Bulgarians enjoy folk music and dancing at parties and feasts.

At these celebrations, people often wear traditional clothing. The women wear an embroidered blouse, one or two aprons, and a belt. Men wear either a white or black tunic. Over this, they may wear a sleeveless jacket and a cloak. Men's pants are belted and can be baggy or tight.

These Bulgarians are wearing traditional clothing and performing a line dance called the **Horo**.

Much of Bulgaria's early artwork was lost when the **Ottoman Empire** took over. But, arts began to grow again in the 1800s. Zahari Zograph and Hristo Tsokev became well known for their paintings. Anton Mitov painted the daily life of the Bulgarian people.

In the 1900s, Vladimir Dimitrov painted rural Bulgarian scenery. Ilya Petrov painted historical scenes. After **World War II**, Bulgarian artists developed the **socialist** realism style. Paintings in this style are often historical themes in cartoons, still lifes, and landscapes.

Sports are an important part of Bulgarian **culture**. Bulgarians excel in weight lifting, wrestling, and gymnastics. The country's big sporting event is the National Spartakiad. Individuals, teams, and clubs participate in many sporting activities during this event. Also, watching soccer matches is a favorite Bulgarian pastime.

Bulgarians enjoy life in many ways. The younger generation enjoys movies, books, music, and popular dance from other parts of Europe. The Black Sea is a favorite vacation spot. But overall, being with family and friends is most important.

The Bulgarian Football Union has played in seven World Cup tournaments. Here, players celebrate the team's best finish, a 1994 quarterfinal win over defending champion Germany.

Glossary

Balkan League - an alliance of the governments of Serbia, Romania, Montenegro, Greece, and a Bulgarian revolutionary group. Its goal was to drive the Turks from the Balkans and to unite southern Slavs into a state.

Balkan Wars - from 1912 to 1913. In the first war, the Balkan League defeated the Ottoman Empire, gaining Macedonia. The second war, between members of the league, divided the new land.

basin - the entire region of land drained by a river and its tributaries.

Byzantine - of or relating to the Byzantine Empire, the eastern part of the Roman Empire.

Central powers - countries that fought together during World War I. Germany, Bulgaria, Austria, and the Ottoman Empire were called the Central powers. They fought the Allies.

communism - a social and economic system in which everything is owned by the government and given to the people as needed. A person who believes in communism is called a communist.

constitution - the laws that govern a country.

culture - the customs, arts, and tools of a nation or people at a certain time.

democracy - a governmental system in which the people vote on how to run their country.

dialect - a form of a language spoken in a certain area or by certain people.

economy - the way a nation uses its money, goods, and natural resources.

European Union (EU) - an organization of European countries that works toward political, economic, governmental, and social unity.

folklife - the traditions, activities, skills, and products of a particular people or group. Folk art and folk music are part of a country's folklife.

Great Depression - the period from 1929 to 1942 of worldwide economic trouble when there was little buying or selling, and many people could not find work.

humid - having moisture or dampness in the air.

irrigate - to supply land with water by using channels, streams, and pipes.

khan - a local chieftain or man of authority.

Muslim - a person who follows Islam. Islam is a religion based on the teachings of the prophet Muhammad as they appear in the Koran.

NATO - North Atlantic Treaty Organization. A group formed by the United States, Canada, and some European countries in 1949. It tries to create peace among its nations and protect them from common enemies.

Orthodox - a Christian church that developed from the churches of the Byzantine Empire.

Ottoman Empire - an empire created by Turkish tribes that existed from 1300 to 1922. At its height between the 1600s and 1700s, the empire ruled Europe, northern Africa, and the Arabian Peninsula.

parliament - the highest lawmaking body of some governments.

parliamentary democracy - a form of government in which the decisions of the nation are made by the people through the elected parliament.

socialism - a kind of economy in which either the government or all of the citizens control the production and distribution of goods. A person who believes in socialism is called a socialist.

vocational - relating to training in a skill or a trade to be pursued as a career.

World War I - from 1914 to 1918, fought in Europe. Great Britain, France, Russia, the United States, and their allies were on one side. Germany, Austria-Hungary, and their allies were on the other side.

World War II - from 1939 to 1945, fought in Europe, Asia, and Africa. Great Britain, France, the United States, the Soviet Union, and their allies were on one side. Germany, Italy, Japan, and their allies were on the other side.

Web Sites

To learn more about Bulgaria, visit ABDO Publishing Company on the World Wide Web at **www.abdopublishing.com**. Web sites about Bulgaria are featured on our Book Links page. These links are routinely monitored and updated to provide the most current information available.

Index